THE
STUDENT'S ENTRY
A RECORD BOOK FOR TEACHERS

Activinotes

Activinotes

DAILY JOURNALS, PLANNERS, NOTEBOOKS AND OTHER BLANK BOOKS

Copyright 2016

THIS BOOK

BELONGS TO

_____

This Weeks

School Lesson

Date:

___/___/___

Weekly Schedule for:_____

Subject	Monday	Tuesday	Wednesday	Thursday	Friday

Weekly Lesson Plan

Date	Instructions	Observations

Class:_____																				
	Week:					Week:					Week:					Week:				
Day	M	T	W	Th	F	M	T	W	Th	F	M	T	W	Th	F	M	T	W	Th	F
Date																				
Assignments																				
Name																				

This Weeks

School Lesson

Date:

___/___/___

Weekly Schedule for:_____

Subject	Monday	Tuesday	Wednesday	Thursday	Friday

Weekly Lesson Plan

Date	Instructions	Observations

Class:_____

	Week:					Week:					Week:					Week:				
Day	M	T	W	Th	F	M	T	W	Th	F	M	T	W	Th	F	M	T	W	Th	F
Date																				
Assignments																				
Name																				

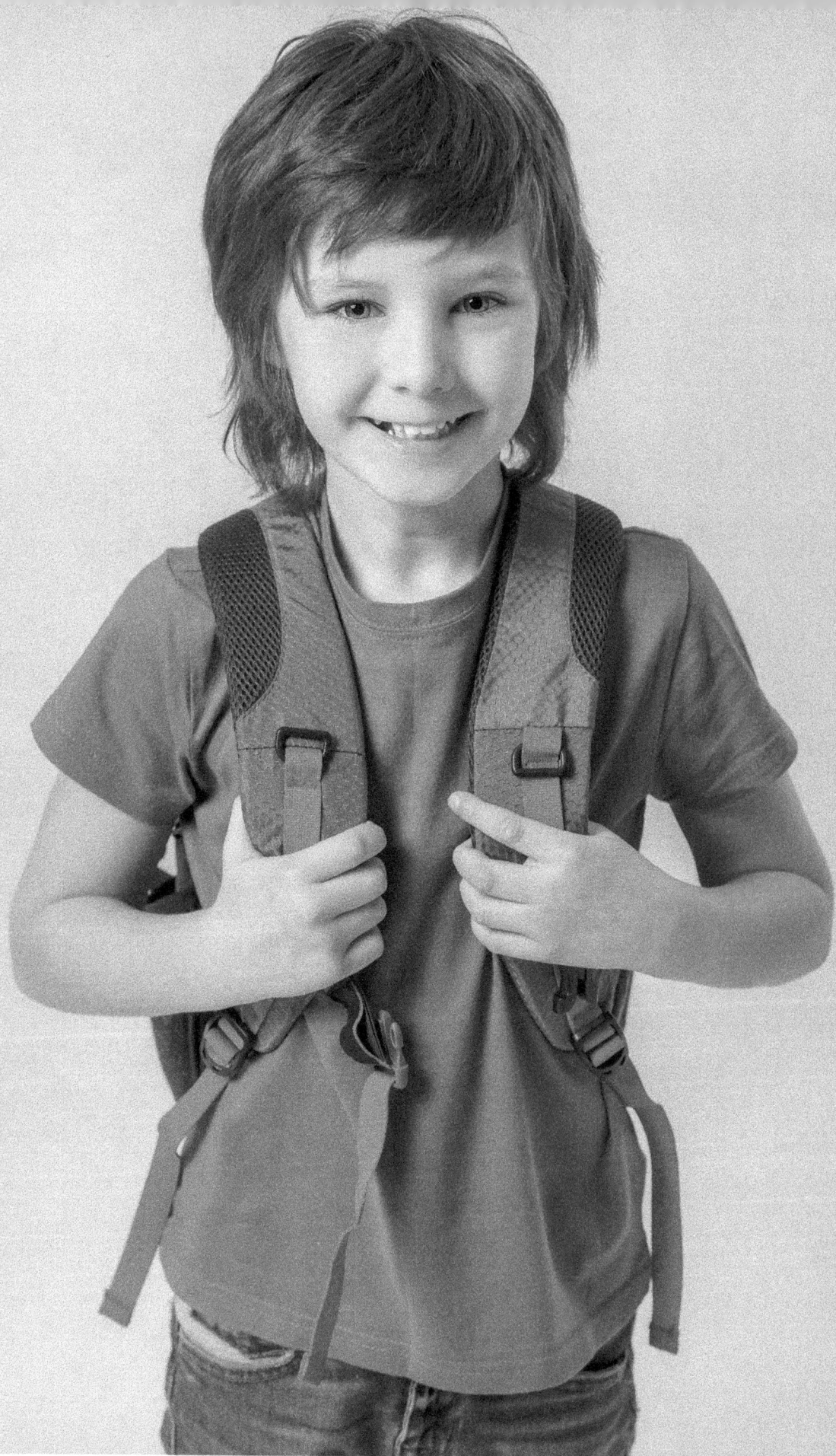

This Weeks

School Lesson

Date:

___/___/___

Weekly Schedule for:_____

Subject	Monday	Tuesday	Wednesday	Thursday	Friday

Weekly Lesson Plan

Date	Instructions	Observations

Class:_____

Day	Week:					Week:					Week:					Week:				
	M	T	W	Th	F	M	T	W	Th	F	M	T	W	Th	F	M	T	W	Th	F
Date																				
Assignments																				
Name																				

This Weeks

School Lesson

Date:

___ / ___ / ___

Weekly Schedule for:_____

Subject	Monday	Tuesday	Wednesday	Thursday	Friday

Weekly Lesson Plan

Date	Instructions	Observations

Class:_____

	Week:					Week:					Week:					Week:				
Day	M	T	W	Th	F	M	T	W	Th	F	M	T	W	Th	F	M	T	W	Th	F
Date																				
Assignments																				
Name																				

This Weeks

School Lesson

Date:

_____/_____/_____

Weekly Schedule for:_____

Subject	Monday	Tuesday	Wednesday	Thursday	Friday

Weekly Lesson Plan

Date	Instructions	Observations

Class:																				
	Week:					Week:					Week:					Week:				
Day	M	T	W	Th	F	M	T	W	Th	F	M	T	W	Th	F	M	T	W	Th	F
Date																				
Assignments																					
Name																					

This Weeks

School Lesson

Date:

___/___/___

Weekly Schedule for:_____

Subject	Monday	Tuesday	Wednesday	Thursday	Friday

Weekly Lesson Plan

Date	Instructions	Observations

Class:																				

	Week:					Week:					Week:					Week:				
Day	M	T	W	Th	F	M	T	W	Th	F	M	T	W	Th	F	M	T	W	Th	F
Date																				
Assignments																				
Name																				

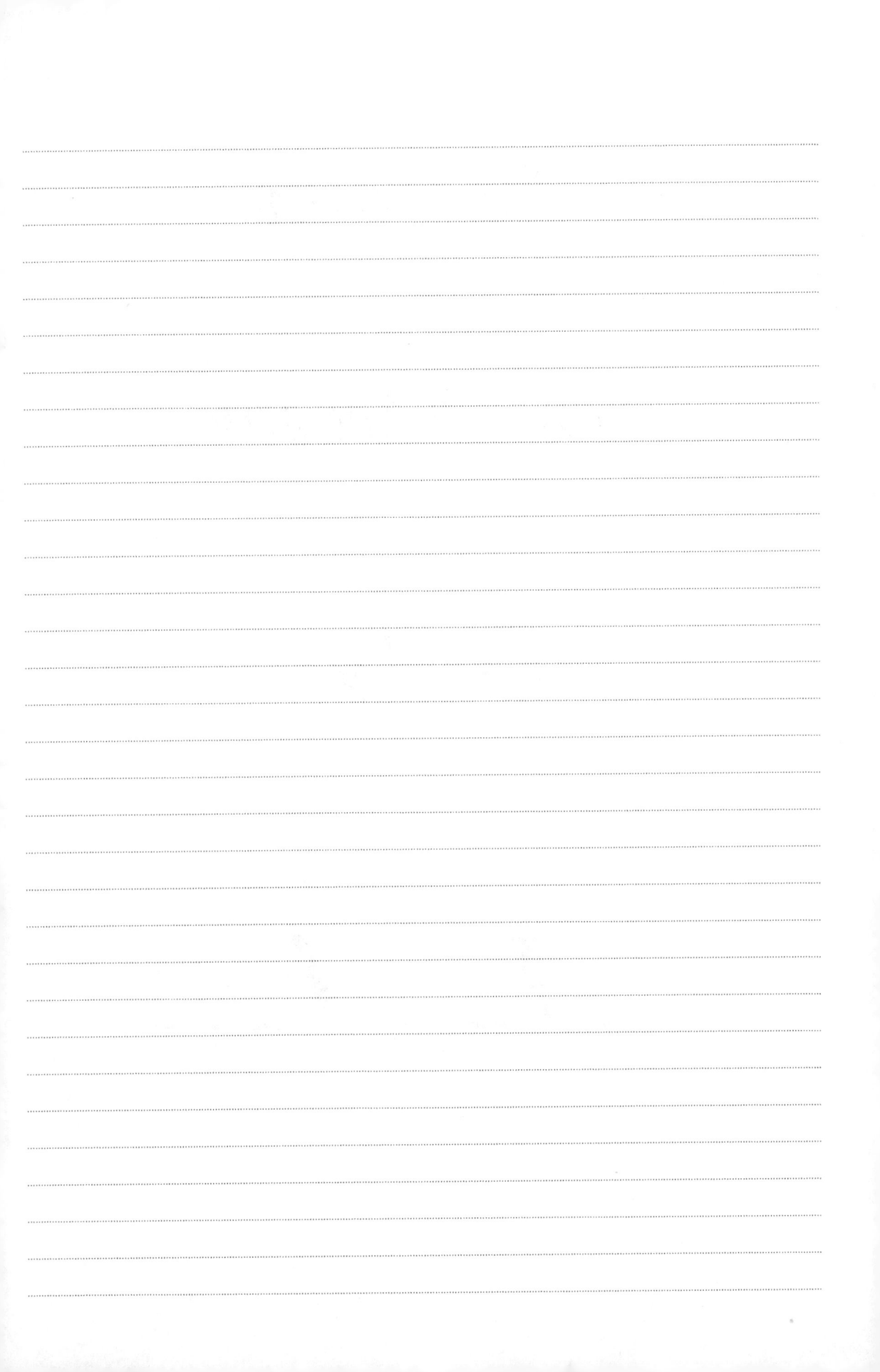

This Weeks

School Lesson

Date:

___/___/___

Weekly Schedule for:_____

Subject	Monday	Tuesday	Wednesday	Thursday	Friday

Weekly Lesson Plan

Date	Instructions	Observations

Class:_____

	Week:					Week:					Week:					Week:				
Day	M	T	W	Th	F	M	T	W	Th	F	M	T	W	Th	F	M	T	W	Th	F
Date																				
Assignments																				
Name																				

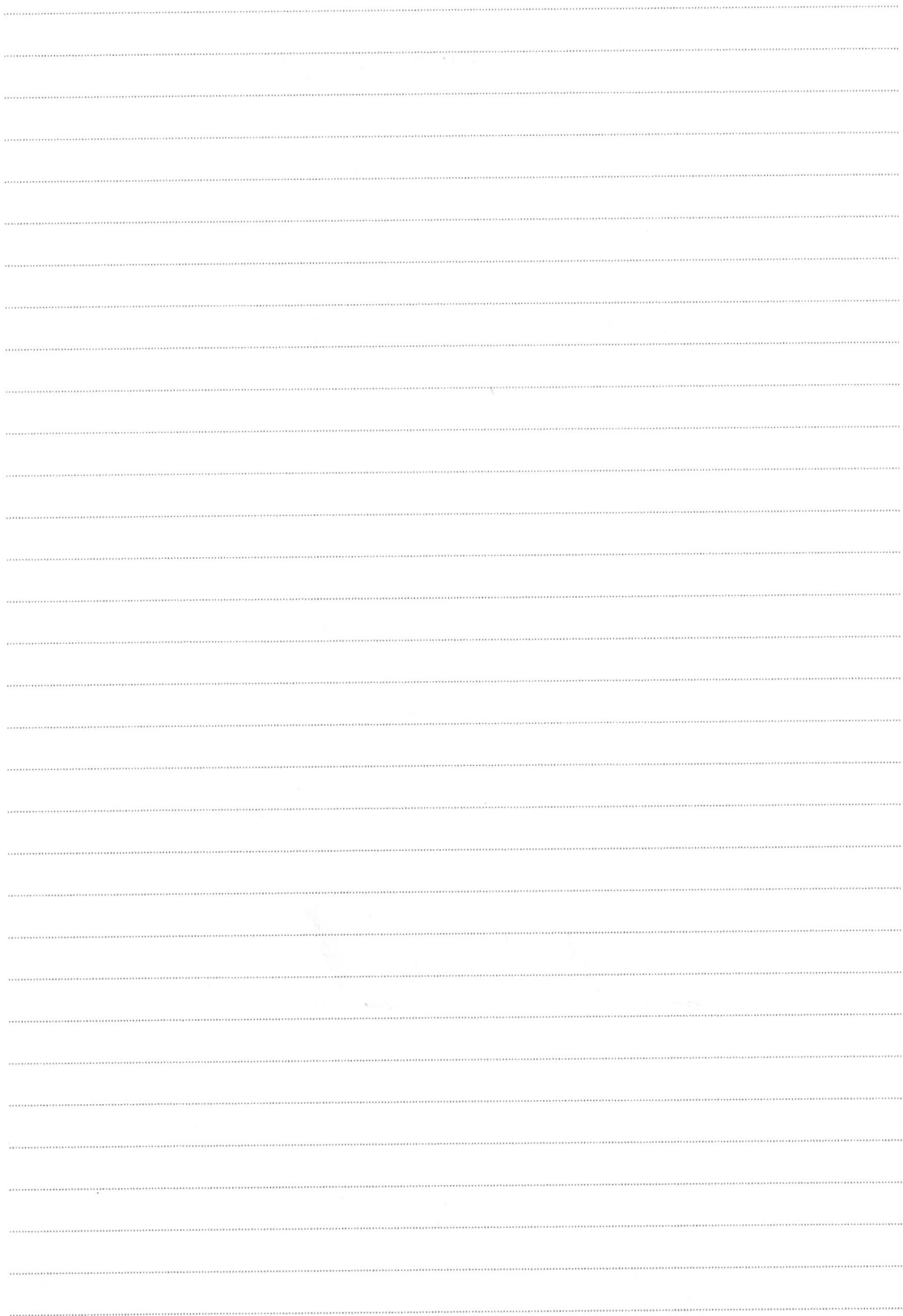

This Weeks

School Lesson

Date:

___/___/___

Weekly Schedule for:_____

Subject	Monday	Tuesday	Wednesday	Thursday	Friday

Weekly Lesson Plan

Date	Instructions	Observations

Class:																				

	Week:					Week:					Week:					Week:				
Day	M	T	W	Th	F	M	T	W	Th	F	M	T	W	Th	F	M	T	W	Th	F
Date																				
Assignments																				
Name																				

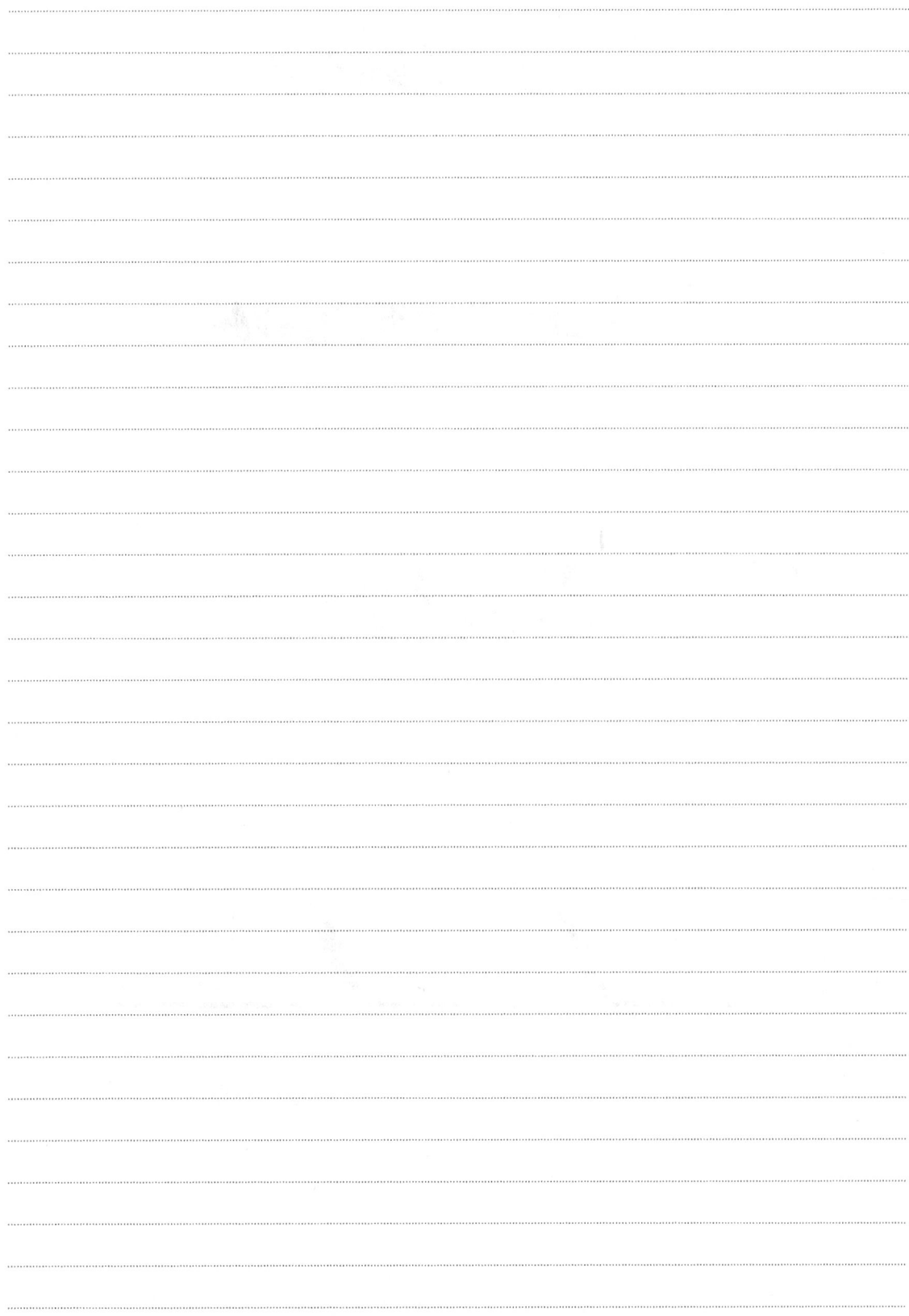

This Weeks

School Lesson

Date:

___/___/___

Weekly Schedule for:_____

Subject	Monday	Tuesday	Wednesday	Thursday	Friday

Weekly Lesson Plan

Date	Instructions	Observations

Class:																				

	Week:					Week:					Week:					Week:				
Day	M	T	W	Th	F	M	T	W	Th	F	M	T	W	Th	F	M	T	W	Th	F
Date																				
Assignments																				
Name																				

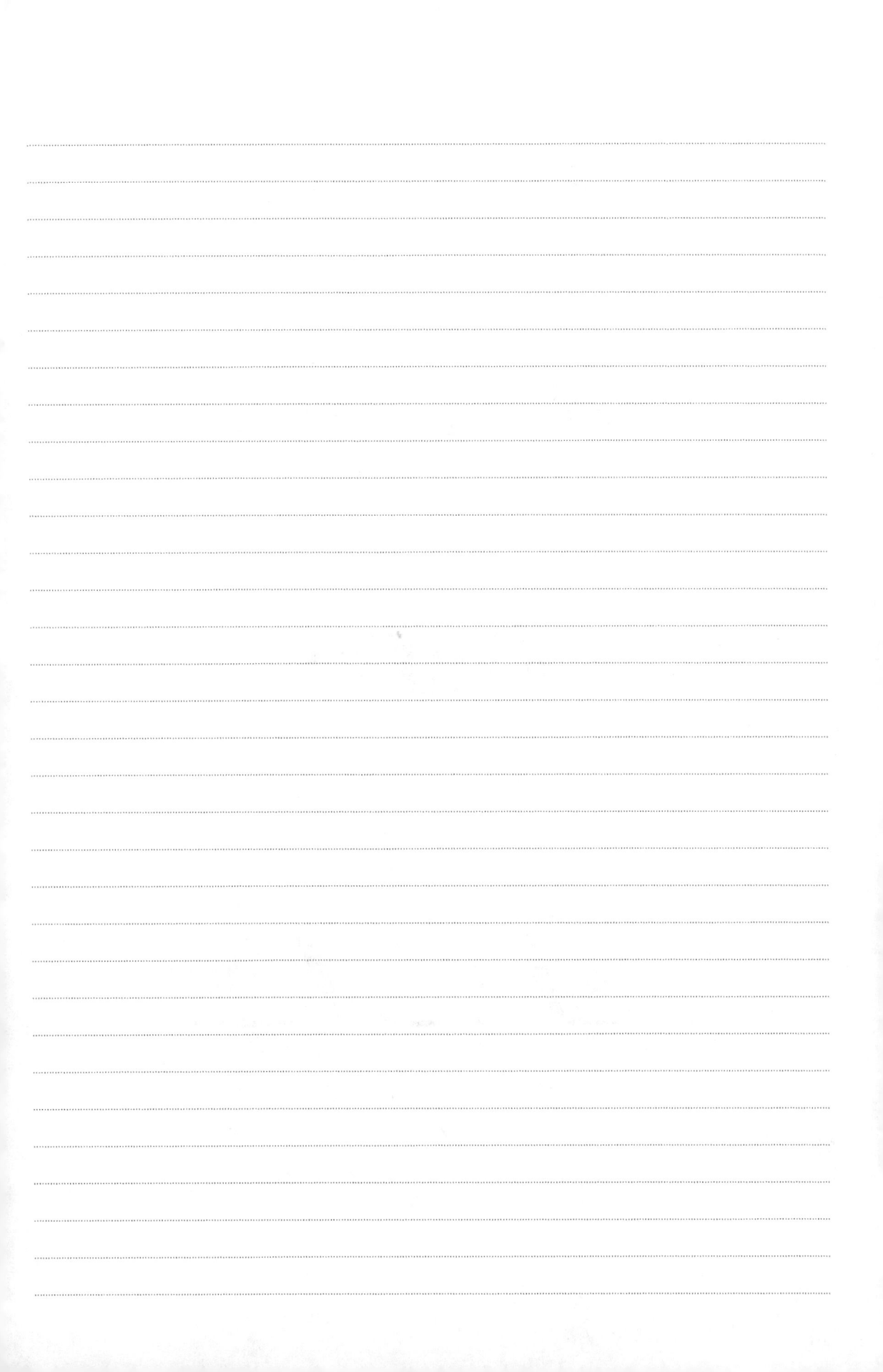

This Weeks

School Lesson

Date:

___/___/___

Weekly Schedule for:＿＿＿＿＿＿＿＿＿＿

Subject	Monday	Tuesday	Wednesday	Thursday	Friday

Weekly Lesson Plan

Date	Instructions	Observations

Class:																				
	Week:					Week:					Week:					Week:				
Day	M	T	W	Th	F	M	T	W	Th	F	M	T	W	Th	F	M	T	W	Th	F
Date																				
Assignments																				
Name																				

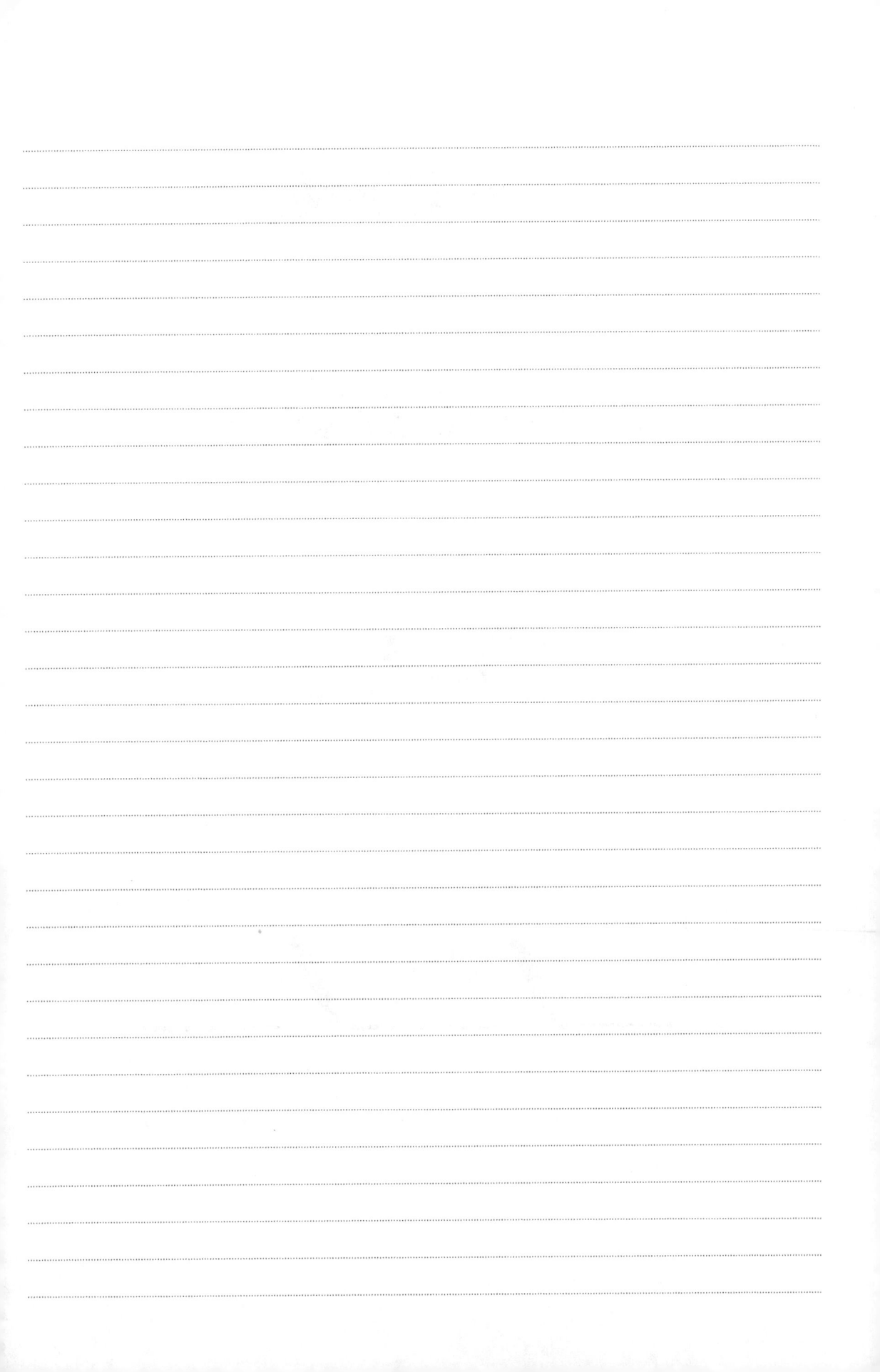

This Weeks

School Lesson

Date:

___ / ___ / ___

Weekly Schedule for:_____

Subject	Monday	Tuesday	Wednesday	Thursday	Friday

Weekly Lesson Plan

Date	Instructions	Observations

Class:																				
	Week:					Week:					Week:					Week:				
Day	M	T	W	Th	F	M	T	W	Th	F	M	T	W	Th	F	M	T	W	Th	F
Date																				
Assignments																				
Name																				

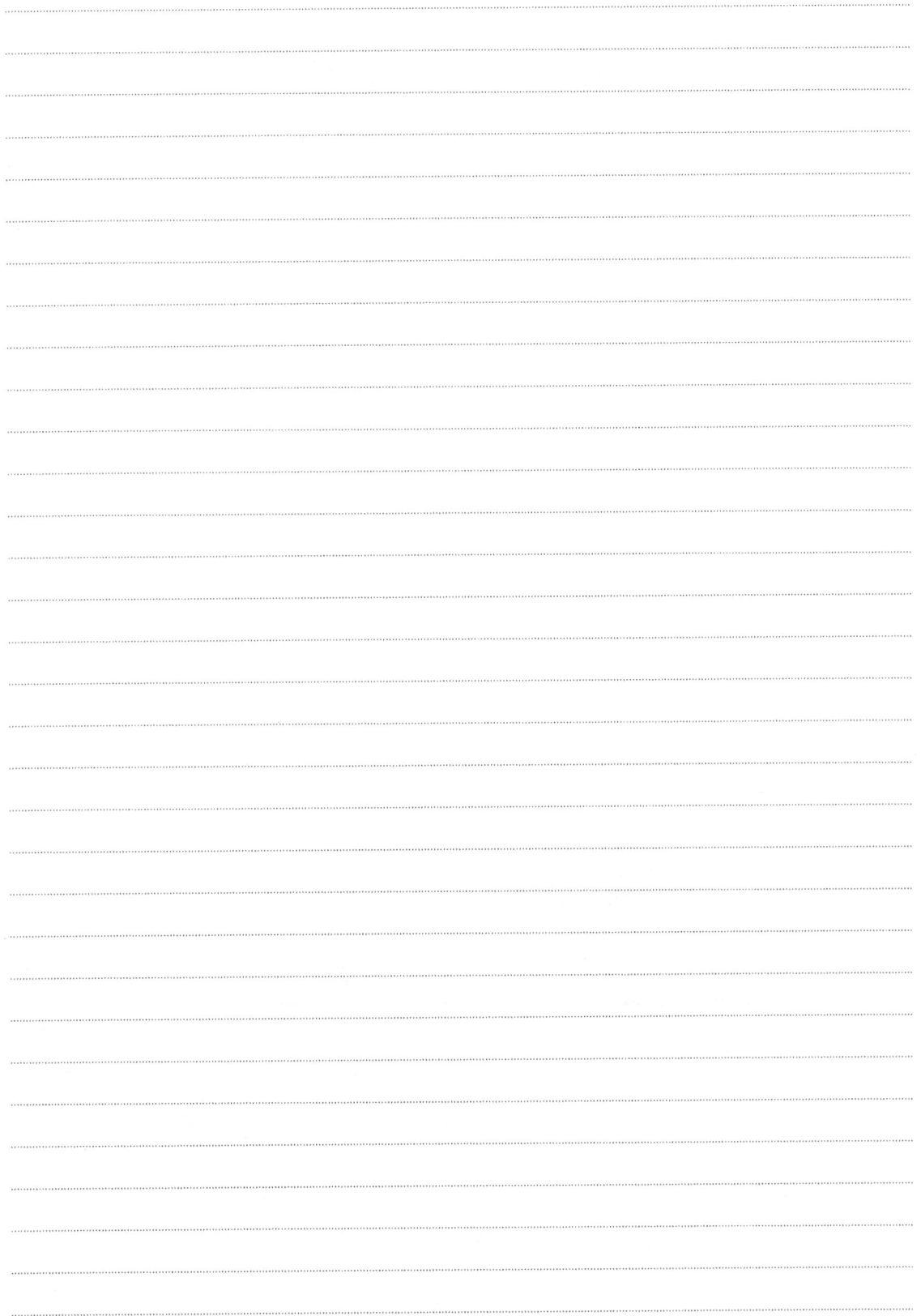

This Weeks

School Lesson

Date:

___/___/___

Weekly Schedule for:_____

Subject	Monday	Tuesday	Wednesday	Thursday	Friday

Weekly Lesson Plan

Date	Instructions	Observations

Class:																				
	Week:					Week:					Week:					Week:				
Day	M	T	W	Th	F	M	T	W	Th	F	M	T	W	Th	F	M	T	W	Th	F
Date																				
Assignments																				
Name																				

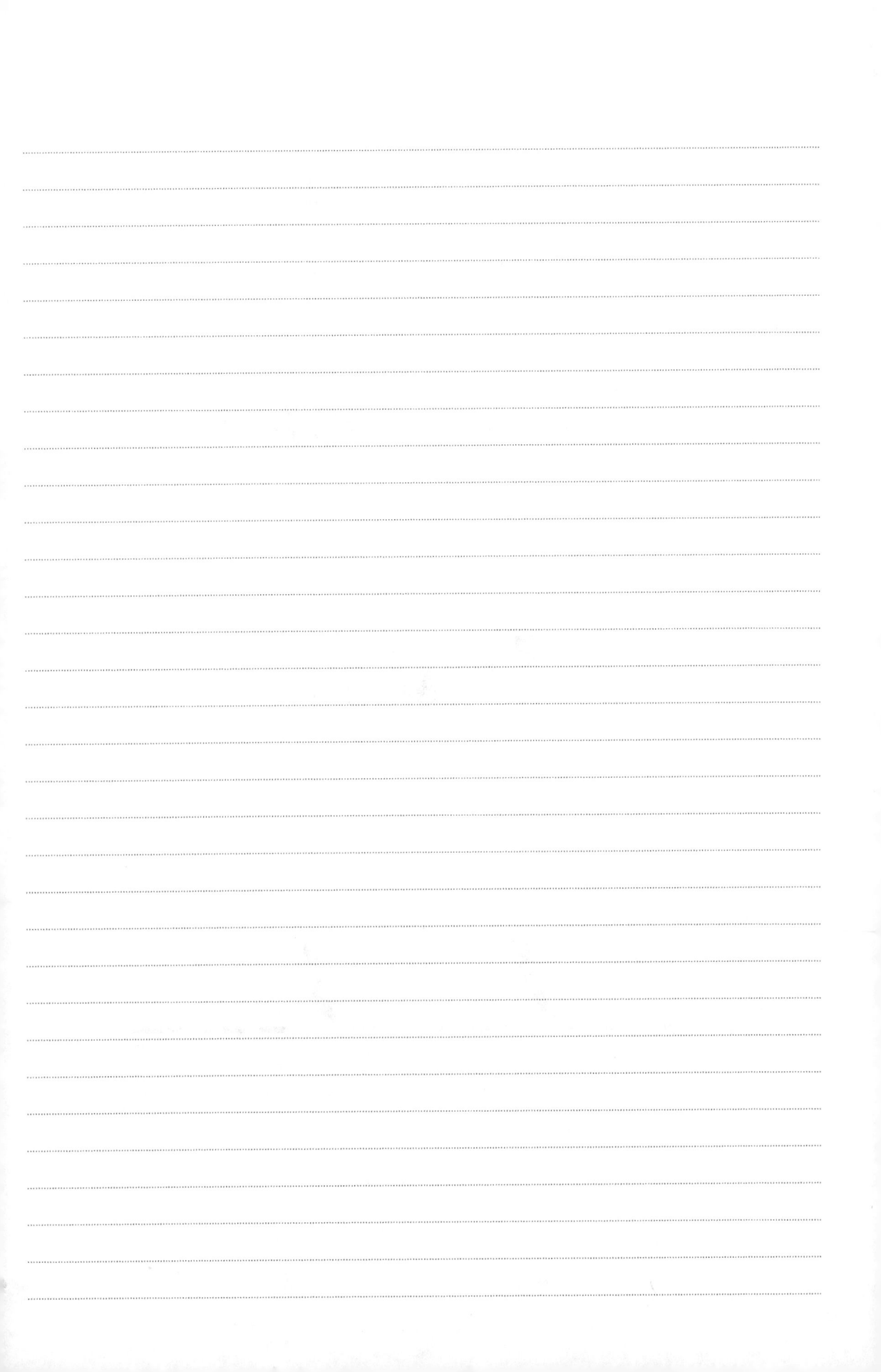

This Weeks

School Lesson

Date:

___/___/___

Weekly Schedule for:_____

Subject	Monday	Tuesday	Wednesday	Thursday	Friday

Weekly Lesson Plan

Date	Instructions	Observations

Class:																				
	Week:					Week:					Week:					Week:				
Day	M	T	W	Th	F	M	T	W	Th	F	M	T	W	Th	F	M	T	W	Th	F
Date																				
Assignments																				
Name																				

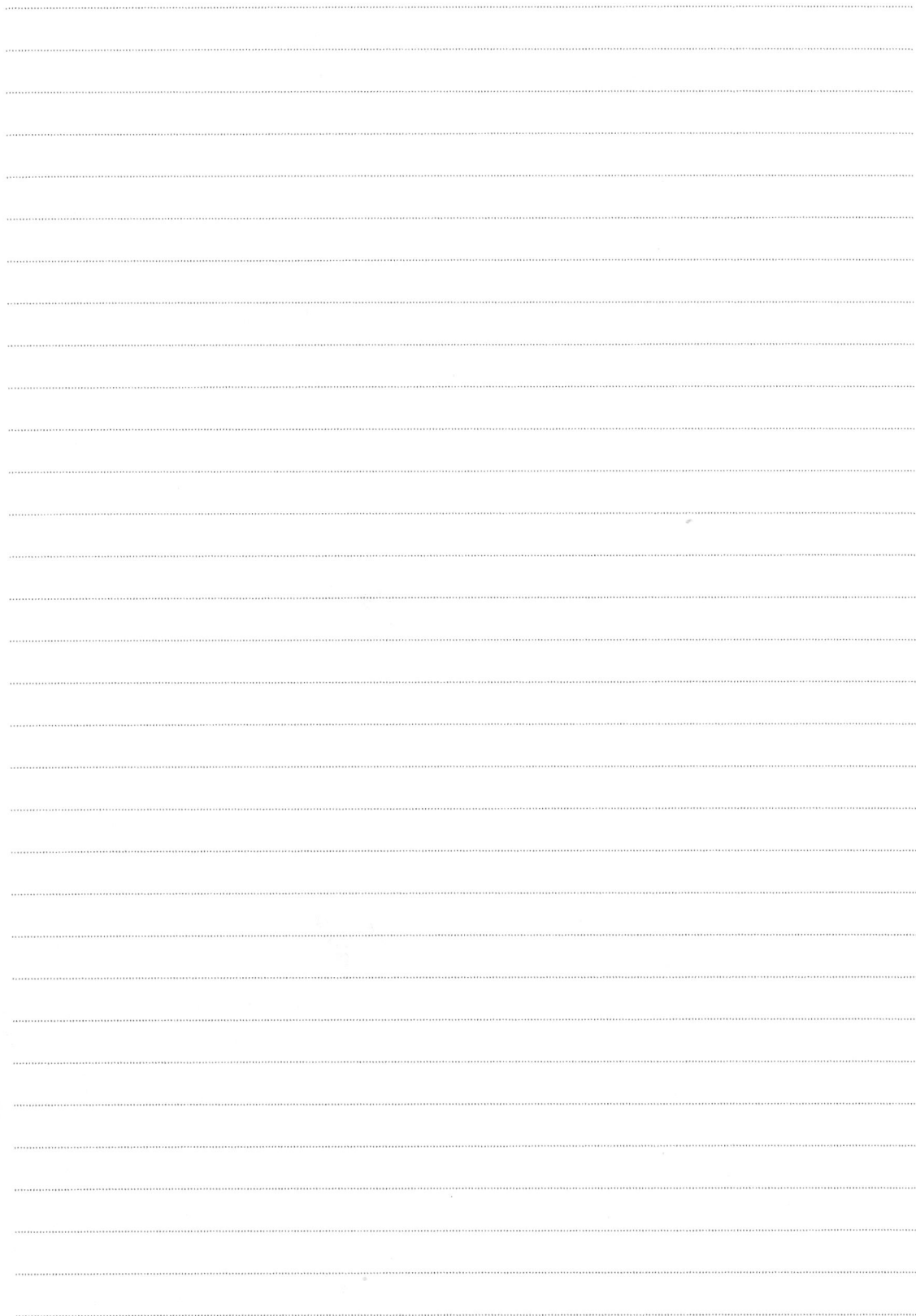

This Weeks

School Lesson

Date:

___/___/___

Weekly Schedule for:_____

Subject	Monday	Tuesday	Wednesday	Thursday	Friday

Weekly Lesson Plan

Date	Instructions	Observations

Class:_____

	Week:					Week:					Week:					Week:				
Day	M	T	W	Th	F	M	T	W	Th	F	M	T	W	Th	F	M	T	W	Th	F
Date																				
Assignments																				
Name																				

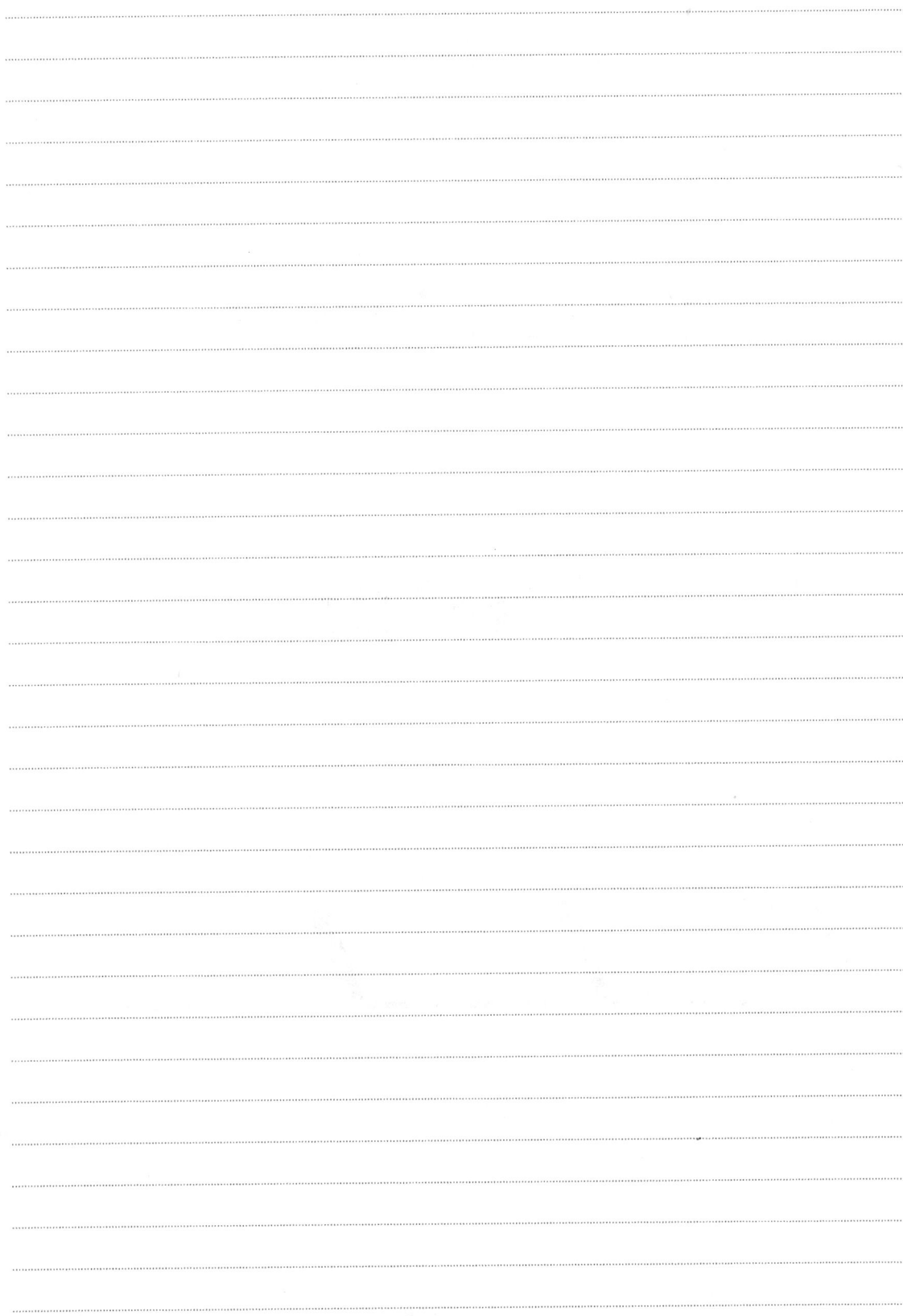

This Weeks

School Lesson

Date:

___/___/___

Weekly Schedule for:_____

Subject	Monday	Tuesday	Wednesday	Thursday	Friday

Weekly Lesson Plan

Date	Instructions	Observations

Class:																				

	Week:					Week:					Week:					Week:				
Day	M	T	W	Th	F	M	T	W	Th	F	M	T	W	Th	F	M	T	W	Th	F
Date																				
Assignments																				
Name																				

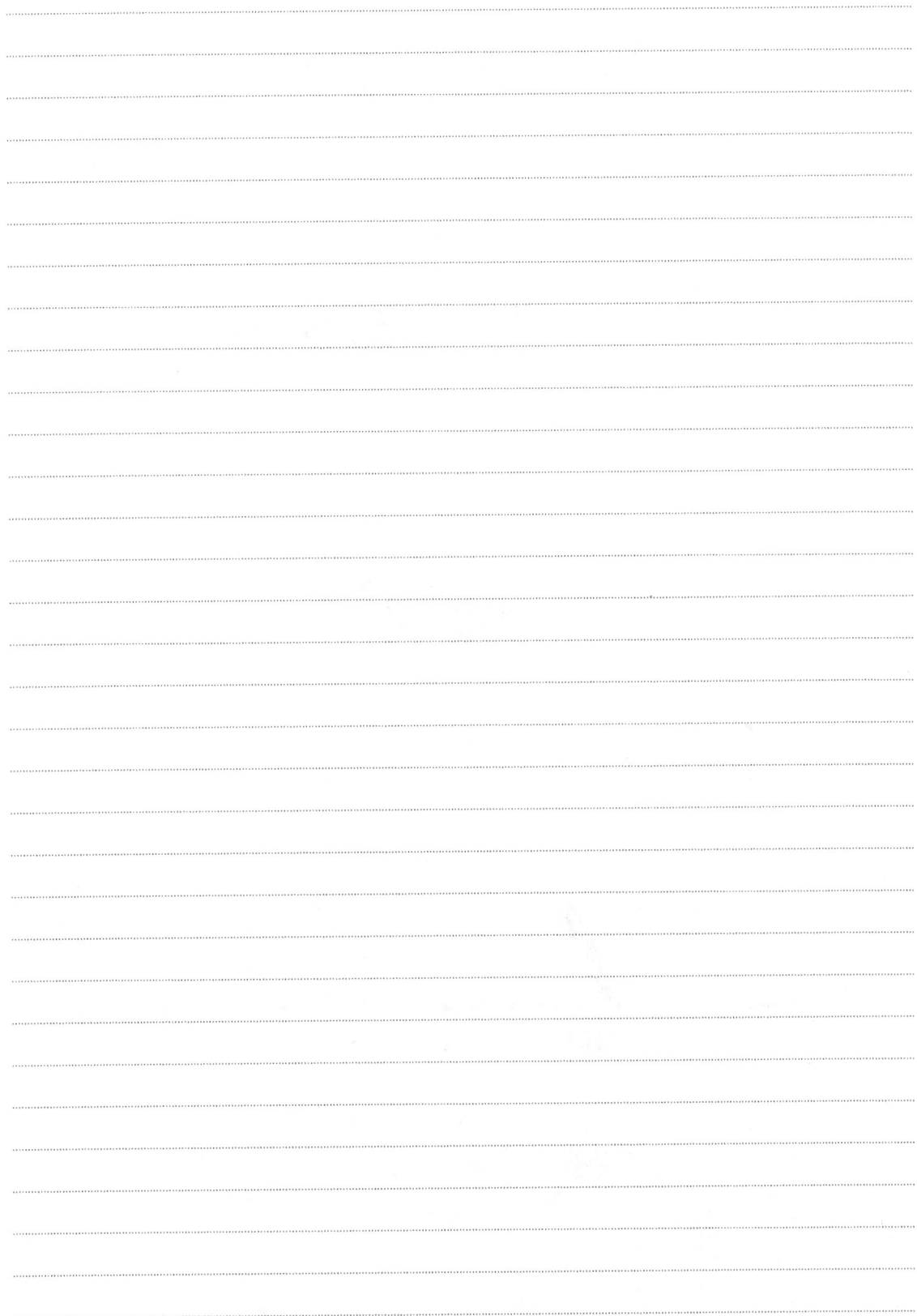

This Weeks

School Lesson

Date:

___/___/___

Weekly Schedule for:_____

Subject	Monday	Tuesday	Wednesday	Thursday	Friday

Weekly Lesson Plan

Date	Instructions	Observations

Class:																				

	Week:					Week:					Week:					Week:				
Day	M	T	W	Th	F	M	T	W	Th	F	M	T	W	Th	F	M	T	W	Th	F
Date																				
Assignments																				
Name																				

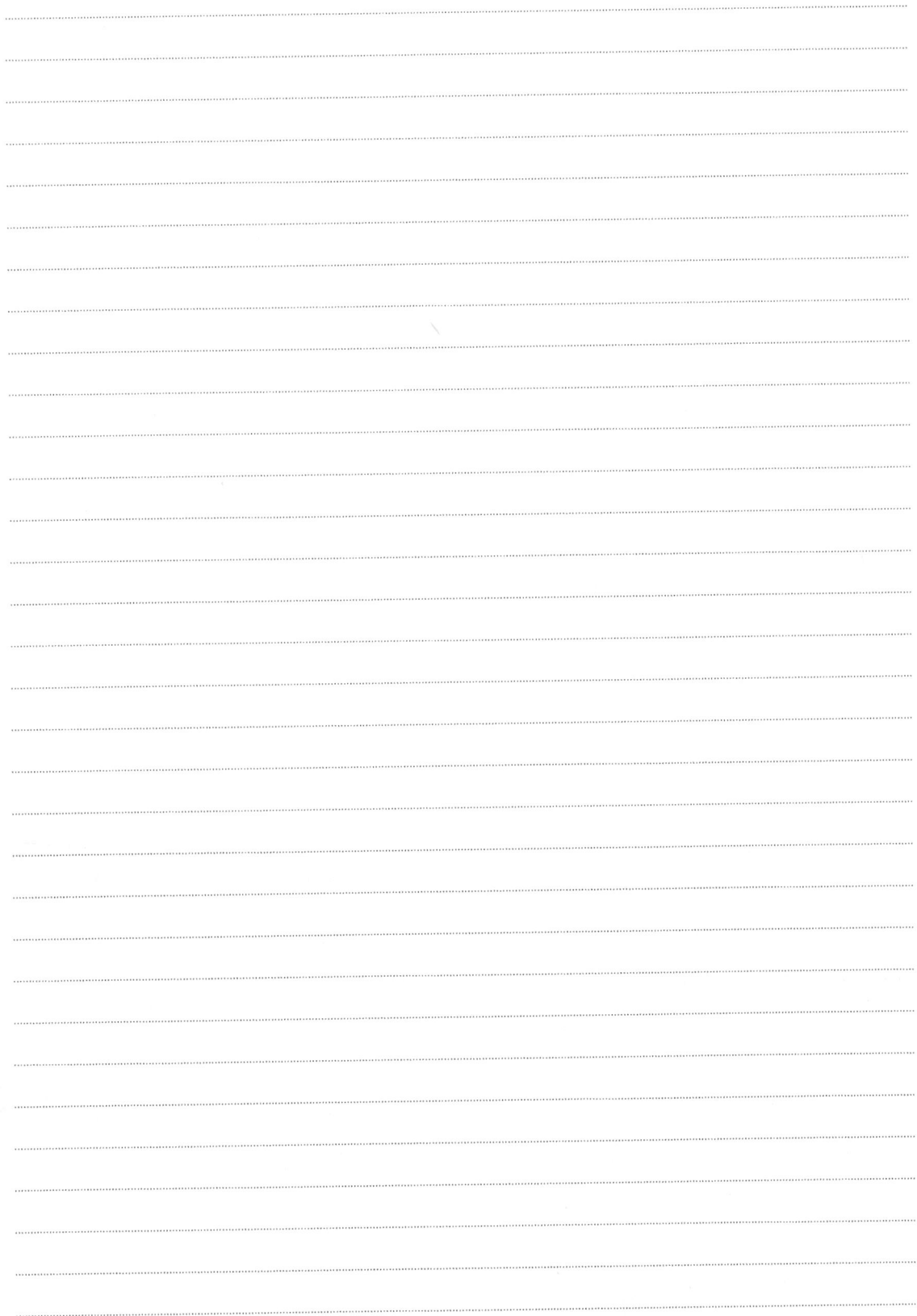

www.ingramcontent.com/pod-product-compliance
Lightning Source LLC
Chambersburg PA
CBHW081338090426
42737CB00017B/3191